This story is dedicated to another magical girl,
the lovely Dlonra (aka Loni).
—N.J.J.

To Mathilda, my daughter:
May your dreams guide you through the paths of life.
—D.E.

Text copyright © 2024 Nancy Johnson James
Illustrations copyright © 2024 Diana Ejaita

Photo from *Thoughts of Idle Hours* by Myra Viola Wilds
(Nashville: National Baptist Publishing Board, 1915).

Book design by Melissa Nelson Greenberg

Published in 2024 by CAMERON KIDS, an imprint of ABRAMS. All rights reserved.
No portion of this book may be reproduced, stored in a retrieval system, or transmitted in
any form or by any means, mechanical, electronic, photocopying, recording, or otherwise,
without written permission from the publisher.

Library of Congress Control Number: 2023947381
ISBN: 978-1-951836-53-5

Printed in China

10 9 8 7 6 5 4 3 2 1

CAMERON KIDS books are available at special discounts when purchased in quantity
for premiums and promotions as well as fundraising or educational use. Special editions
can also be created to specifications. For details, contact specialsales@abramsbooks.com
or the address below.

ABRAMS The Art of Books
195 Broadway, New York, NY 10007
abramsbooks.com

DREAM A DRESS, DREAM A POEM

DRESSMAKER AND POET, MYRA VIOLA WILDS

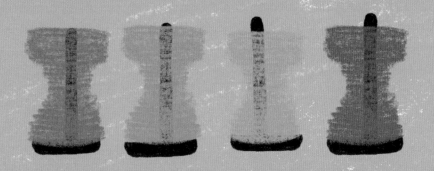

BY NANCY JOHNSON JAMES
ILLUSTRATED BY DIANA EJAITA

cameron kids

"Thoughts" by Myra Viola Wilds

What kind of thoughts now, do you carry
In your travels day by day
Are they bright and lofty visions,
Or neglected, gone astray?

Matters not how great in fancy,
Or what deed of skill you've wrought;
Man, though high may be his station,
Is not better than his thoughts.

Catch your thoughts and hold them tightly,
Let each one an honor be;
Purge them, scourge them, burnish brightly,
Then in love set each one free.

What thoughts do you carry
when idle with nothing to do?
Do you dream of the future?
Or of someone who lived before you?

Dream a world, dream a time
and the story of a girl.
Dream Myra Viola Wilds,
dressmaker long ago.

Dream a place that brings to mind
those green Kentucky hills.
The lush grass, the swaying trees,
where dreams went unfulfilled.

The memories of Myra's home.
The fields and hollers she would roam.
Where people with old-timey ways
sang to keep the blues away.

Dream a sparrow passing by,
flying cross a changing sky.
The raccoon, possum, white-tailed deer,
squirrel, chipmunk, and black bear.

The feelings in Myra's eyes
when she had to say goodbye
and leave that simple country place,
with its past and its pain.

A journey to new opportunity
and more kindness in the city.
The chance to learn and to read,
to be a part of society.

Dream Myra Viola Wilds,
dressmaker long ago.
Sitting sewing gorgeous gowns
and fashionable frocks to wear to town.

Dream fancy, frilly, even funny,
looking sweet like flowery honey.
Formal for important places,
big ideas, and serious faces.

Dream of cotton, lace, or linen,
a dress in wool, silk, or satin,
simply solid, print, or dotted,
showy ruffles, puffs, or pleated.

Sweet-corn yellow, cerulean blue,
purple, green, or varied hues,
the color of your favorite flower,
the feeling of your idle hours.

Delicate work late at night,
the strain in Myra's eyes,
causing damage to her sight,
over time becoming blind.

Dream Myra sitting alone,
new dreams coming to her as poems.
In the darkest hour of night,
penning a poem about sunshine.

Dream a poem, dream a poet
writing the world from memory,
her heart always trusting,
her hands always creating.

Dream a dress that is a poem,
like Myra would have made.
Words with color, form, and song.
Lines stitched short, curved, and long.

Dream a dream when you struggle,
between a painful past and a hopeful tomorrow.
Remember when light began to fade,
Myra's art could still be made.

Catch your dreams and hold them lightly.
Free your hands and create each day.
Your dreamwork shining brightly,
set like gems along the way.

ABOUT MYRA VIOLA WILDS

Myra Viola Wilds lived during an "in-between" time in US history. Reconstruction (the period after the Civil War) had ended, and the Harlem Renaissance had not yet begun. This was a time when Black people lived with unusual tensions. Most of Myra Viola Wild's peers would have been born to people who were enslaved. They would have survived the Civil War, celebrated Emancipation, participated in politics during reconstruction, and then often faced cruel and violent backlash.

White citizens who had wanted to continue enslaving Black people tried to "redeem" what they lost during the Civil War. They did not want equality for newly freed Black people. They wanted the power and wealth they felt they had before the war, which they had gained from the labor they exploited. They created a legal framework rooted in racism that allowed them to maintain a way of life that was separate and unequal.

This legal framework, constructed of legislation called Jim Crow laws, caused a great deal of hardship for Black people and other people of color. Having been born and raised in Kentucky, Myra would have experienced life under Jim Crow. She would have encountered whites-only buildings and been denied access to basic services.

But those hardships are only a fraction of Myra's story. People who believed in justice did not give up. Black communities and others who believed in fairness built schools and colleges so that Black people could have the opportunity to learn the skills they needed to succeed. They also created organizations to advocate for the community and started their own newspapers and magazines. These people did their best to establish all the businesses and institutions that the Black community needed.

Myra's book of poems, *Thoughts of Idle Hours*, was published by the National Baptist Publishing Board in Nashville, Tennessee, in 1915. This enterprise was founded by a group of Black businesspeople who wanted to publish work created by Black writers and to make those materials available to the Black community. Myra's poems were also included in an anthology by Effie T. Battle called *Six Poets of Racial Uplift*. This book presented poetry by Black women who shared their thoughts, advocated for themselves, and worked toward the advancement of the community.

Myra was born in a small town in Kentucky that she called Mount Ollie, which might have referred to either Mount Olive, Kentucky, or Mount Olivet, Kentucky; at the time she was born, people who were poor did not have many records to document their lives. She was not able to get an education in her town. So, she went to a place where she could learn to read. She also learned to be a dressmaker.

That she most likely left her home to find access to opportunities was not unusual. Many Black people traveled far away from their hometowns and families, in what became known as the Great Migration, to go to school, find work, or start businesses. Myra Viola Wilds was a part of this strong community. Even though Black citizens faced many challenges, they continued to have great hope for the future.

Dressmaking was a special profession before the mass production of clothing. Myra designed and made beautiful clothes for women. This was slow and time-consuming, as dressmakers did very intricate work, and making clothes took many long hours. Most people didn't have many clothes, so they needed the ones they had to be well made. Myra's dressmaking work caused great eye strain, and eventually she lost her sight and became blind. Still Myra did not give up her creativity. She had ideas she wanted to share, so she began to write poems.

As a dressmaker Myra had very skilled hands, along with her sharp and creative mind. She was able to continue writing even though she could not see. Because she was part of a community, she was able to connect with people who could support her work and share her creativity.

"Dewdrops"
by Myra Viola Wilds

Watch the dewdrops in the morning,
Shake their little diamond heads,
Sparkling, flashing, ever moving,
From their silent little beds.

See the grass! Each blade is brightened,
Roots are strengthened by their stay;
Like the dewdrops, let us scatter
Gems of love along the way.

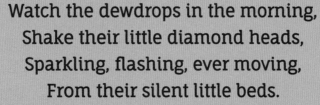
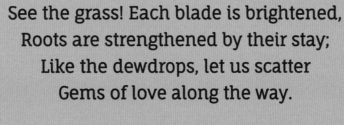